Children of the
PHILIPPINES

THE WORLD'S CHILDREN

Children of the PHILIPPINES

PHOTOGRAPHS BY ELAINE LITTLE
TEXT BY SHEILA KINKADE

Carolrhoda Books, Inc./Minneapolis

We are grateful to the Children and Youth Foundation of the Philippines for introducing us to the many programs and people that are making a positive and lasting difference in young lives throughout the Philippines. —E. L. & S. K.

The publisher wishes to thank Ms. Johanna Buwalda and Mr. Florencio K. Coronel for their generous assistance in the preparation of this book.

Carolrhoda Books, Inc. c/o The Lerner Group
241 First Avenue North, Minneapolis, MN 55401

LIBRARY OF CONGRESS CATALOGING-IN-PUBLICATION DATA

Kinkade, Sheila.
  Children of the Philippines / by Sheila Kinkade ; photographs by Elaine Little.
    p. cm. — (World's children)
  Includes index.
  ISBN 0-87614-993-X
  1. Philippines—Social life and customs—Juvenile literature.
2. Children—Philippines—Social life and customs—Juvenile literature.
I. Little, Elaine, 1958–   ill. II. Title. III. Series: World's children
(Minneapolis, Minn.)
DS663.K5 1995
959.9–dc20   95-34938

Manufactured in the United States of America
1 2 3 4 5 6 – JR – 01 00 99 98 97 96

In the early morning, a thick mist hovers over the Sagada terraces in the northern Philippines. Row after row of rice covers the steep hillsides. Thousands of years ago, mountain farmers created the terraces for the growing of rice.

Jane is eleven years old and lives in a small village in the Sagada terraces. She and her mother, Nali, have been awake for several hours to avoid having to walk in the hot midday sun. Jane carefully balances a basket of green peppers on top of her head as she makes her way down a path to the town of Sagada. She and her mother will sell the peppers in Sagada's outdoor market.

The rice terraces of Sagada are located on the Philippine island of Luzon. The Philippines is a country made up of more than 7,100 islands in Southeast Asia. More than half of these islands are so small they have never been named.

Rice terraces cover more than 100 square miles on the Philippine island of Luzon.

Jane and her mother carry green peppers to the Sagada market.

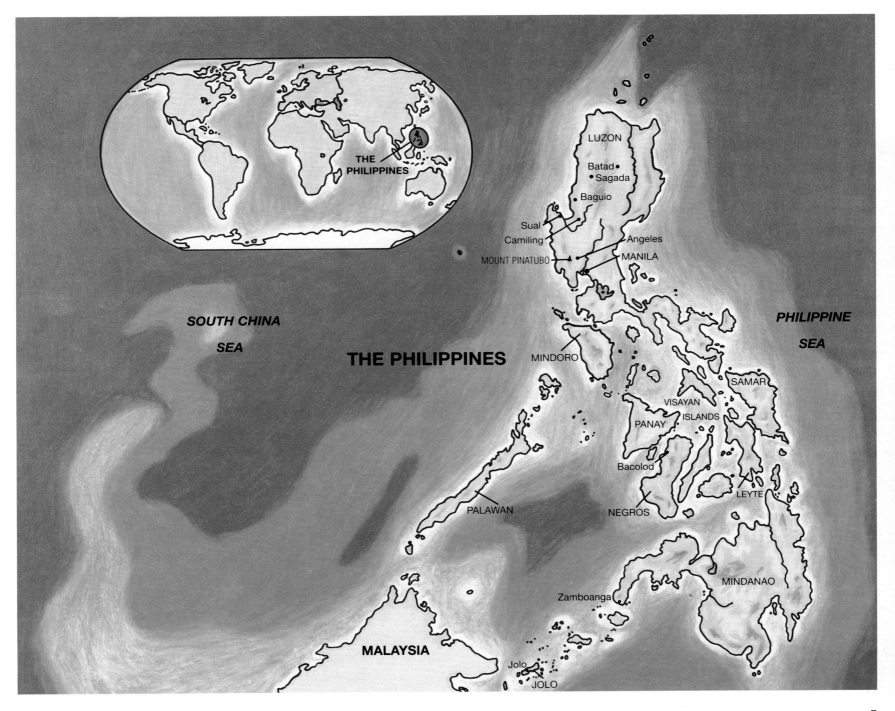

THE PHILIPPINES

THE
PHILIPPINES

LUZON

Batad •
• Sagada

• Baguio

Sual
Camiling
MOUNT PINATUBO →

Angeles
MANILA

SOUTH CHINA
SEA

PHILIPPINE
SEA

MINDORO

SAMAR

VISAYAN
ISLANDS

PANAY

Bacolod

LEYTE

PALAWAN

NEGROS

MINDANAO

Zamboanga

MALAYSIA

Jolo
JOLO

Volcanic activity beneath the ocean floor created the Philippine Islands millions of years ago. What we now call the Philippines is really a vast mountain range, most of which is hidden underwater.

Thousands of years ago, settlers came from Asia to the Philippines. Many of them traveled in boats called *barangays*. The people aboard each boat settled their own villages. Small communities throughout the country are still known as *barangays*.

The first European explorer in the Philippine Islands was Ferdinand Magellan, who sailed on behalf of Spain. Not long after his arrival in 1521, Magellan was killed by Lapulapu, a local chief. In the following years, more Spanish settlers came to the Philippines. In 1565 they claimed the islands and named the new country after King Philip of Spain.

The first European in the Philippines, Ferdinand Magellan was searching for a westward route to Indonesia's spice islands.

Above, opposite page: *A wide variety of Catholic churches can be found in cities, towns, and villages throughout the Philippines. Some churches also serve as libraries or town halls.*

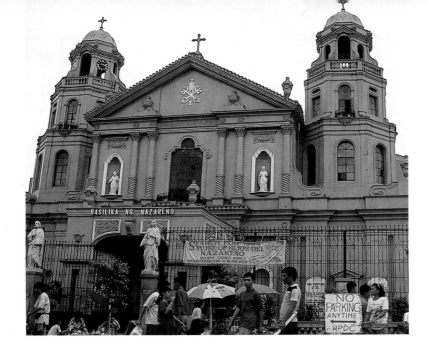

Spain continued to rule the Philippines for the next 333 years. In 1898 the United States took control of the country after the Spanish-American War. Finally, in 1946, the Philippines gained its independence.

Spanish settlers brought the Roman Catholic religion to Filipinos (people who live in the Philippines). About 85 percent of all Filipinos are Catholic. About 5 percent are Muslims, or followers of Islam. The Philippines also has many Protestants.

Ramir helps his mother at the Hillside Inn in Batad.

Ramir and his family live in Batad, a mountain village on the island of Luzon. No roads lead to Batad, so visitors must walk for about two hours through lush trails and up steep steps to reach the village.

Ramir's father is the principal of a school in the town of Banaue. Because he must walk a great distance to get to work, Ramir's father comes home only on weekends. Ramir helps his mother prepare and serve food at the Hillside Inn, the family's restaurant.

When Ramir was very young, his brother threw a stone that accidentally hit Ramir in the eye. His father took Ramir on a long journey to Manila, the capital of the Philippines. He stayed in Manila for almost a month to be treated by an eye doctor. Ramir is the only member of his village who wears glasses.

Ramir

Most people in Batad work in the rice terraces that surround their homes.

Ramir and his friends play basketball on a court they made themselves.

In this Ifugao dance, Ramir and his friends ask an imaginary hawk to scare away any mice or insects that might damage local crops.

The girls of Batad perform a traditional Ifugao dance.

Ramir belongs to the Ifugao tribal group. Many different tribal groups exist throughout the Philippines. Each has its own language, music, clothing, and traditions. Ramir speaks both English and his native language of Ifugao. At school, he studies English and Pilipino, the national language of the Philippines.

Like many children in the Philippines, Ramir spends much of his free time playing basketball. Even in small villages, young people create their own basketball courts. To make a hoop, they use a piece of metal or an old tire and tie it high on a pole—or even a palm tree. Many children decorate their walls with posters of American basketball players.

When travelers from other parts of the Philippines visit Batad, Ramir and his friends perform traditional dances. Handed down through generations, each dance tells a story.

13

In Sual, a coastal village south of Batad, Maricar carefully untangles the strands of a large fishing net. Every morning before school, she helps her father get their boat ready. Sometimes she goes fishing with her father and brother. The long narrow boat, called a *banca,* has two bamboo "arms," which help to balance it in the water.

Fishing is a strong tradition in the Philippines. It is also a major source of income for many Filipino families who live on the coast. Maricar's father must work long hours to catch enough fish to feed his family and to have some to sell at a roadside stand. Fish is often cooked over hot coals and served whole with rice.

Maricar helps her father prepare their fishing nets.

At the end of the day, fishers hang their nets from bamboo poles.

People sell fish at this roadside stand, just a short walk from Maricar's boat.

Nicanor's brother uses the family carabao, or water buffalo, to plow the fields.

Filipinos eat rice at nearly every meal. Most often it is steamed and served piled high on a plate. Rice can also be cooked with garlic, molded into rice cakes, or made into sweet, sticky desserts.

Nicanor and his brothers and sisters live in the central plains of Luzon, a rich agri-cultural area. They help plant and harvest rice and other crops. Throughout the Philippines, farmers grow rice in fields called paddies.

Rice paddies are flooded with water during the grow-ing season. After rice is har-vested by hand, it is dried in the sun. Then farmers take their rice crop to a mill, where special machines re-move the rough outer layers. The rice is then ready for market.

Other crops grown in the Philippines include bananas, pineapples, coconuts, and sugarcane. More than half of all Filipinos live in rural areas and make their living by farming.

Filipinos can buy many different kinds of rice at markets.

Farmers often leave their harvested rice on a street to dry.

After a hard day of work, Nicanor relaxes on the back of the carabao while it grazes.

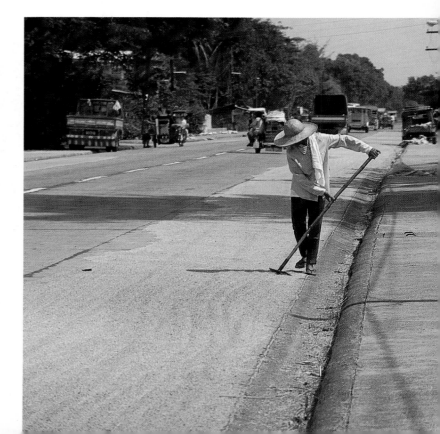

In addition to growing crops, many children in the Philippines help raise farm animals. Ramonito and José live in a small village on the island of Negros. Before and after school, Ramonito cares for his family's cow, which can be quite stubborn.

José's family raises goats and chickens. Every morning, José gets up early to feed the goats and take them out to a field to graze. José's family breeds the goats and sells their offspring.

After working in the sun all morning, young people from a nearby village enjoy a cool dip in a mountain stream. Children of farming families usually own few toys or games, but they easily entertain themselves outdoors. Sometimes they make slingshots out of tree branches or kites from plastic grocery bags.

When the cow stops for a drink on the way back to the family farm, Ramonito must pull extra hard.

José takes care of his family's goats.

18

Many Filipino children are good at making toys from everyday things.

After a day spent working in the fields, these children enjoy a swim.

The city of Baguio sits in the mountains on the island of Luzon. Mariliza stays in Baguio at a shelter for children. The shelter provides a temporary home for children who once lived or worked on the city's busy streets.

In cities throughout the Philippines, many poor children work on the streets to help support their families. Others leave home altogether. To make money, they wash cars, sell candy or vegetables, carry shopping bags for adults, or take on other small jobs.

Like most of the children who stay at this shelter, Mariliza returns to her family's home over the weekend. She lives at the shelter during the week so she can go to school, get help with her studies, eat regular meals, and play with other children.

Many poor children in Filipino cities work to help their families. Above: *Some children stop people in passing cars to sell them newspapers.* Opposite page: *Others sell fish or vegetables in the market.*

An older boy helps Mariliza with a craft project.

Alfredo practices tae kwon do once a week.

In the afternoons at the shelter, Alfredo plays basketball or practices tae kwon do with other boys. Tae kwon do is a Korean martial art that resembles karate. For Alfredo and his friends, their weekly workouts are both fun and serious business. The tough practice drills help teach them discipline.

Mariliza and other girls also practice important skills. Sometimes they work on dances they perform on special occasions. Their brightly colored, traditional clothing is made from hand-woven fabrics. One of the girls' favorite dances describes the tribal groups living in the mountains to the north.

For special events, children at the shelter perform traditional dances.

Girls at the shelter proudly display their traditional outfits.

Many Filipinos leave rural areas in search of jobs and greater opportunities in the city. Manila, the largest city in the Philippines and the nation's capital, draws thousands of new settlers each year. Manila has many fast-food restaurants, shopping malls, and office buildings. This fast-growing city is home to many of the Philippines' wealthiest people, as well as its poorest.

Marivec lives in Manila and hopes to be a police officer someday. Like many Filipinos, she has relatives who live in the United States. American music, fashion, movies, and culture are popular in Manila and other urban areas in the Philippines. While many Filipinos accept the influence of the United States, others seek to preserve their country's unique cultural heritage.

Most people in Manila get around in brightly painted taxis called jeepneys. Filipinos made jeepneys from U.S. Army jeeps left in their country after World War II.

Manila is one of the biggest cities in the world, with over ten million people in its metropolitan area.

Many poor families in Manila live in shacks made from wood and metal scraps.

Marivec

On a hot June day in 1991, the sky over Manila grew dark with thick black clouds, and a fine white dust rained down on the city's streets. Mount Pinatubo, a volcano 90 miles north of Manila, erupted with tremendous force, producing tons of lava, ash, and smoke. Hundreds of people in the surrounding area were killed. A thick blanket of gray ash covered farmland around the mountain.

Nora lives outside the town of Angeles, near Mount Pinatubo. She and her friends sometimes play in abandoned houses damaged by the volcano. For years after the eruption, the volcano continued to produce smoke and ash.

The eruption of Mount Pinatubo was just one of the many natural disasters Filipinos have endured. Typhoons, or very heavy rains, strike the islands each year during the rainy season. Earthquakes occasionally shake the islands.

Mount Pinatubo erupted in June 1991. More than 100 volcanoes dot the Philippine Islands. About 20 of them are active.

Rainstorms sometimes bring wet ash down into towns and villages around Mount Pinatubo. When the ash dries, it is like dust. People cover their faces and try to keep the streets clean.

Nora holds her younger sister in front of their house. Behind them are piles of gray volcanic ash.

The eruption of Mount Pinatubo destroyed thousands of homes. Many of the people left homeless were members of the Aeta tribal group. For centuries, the Aeta had lived as hunters and gatherers in the mountain jungles surrounding the volcano.

After the eruption, many Aeta families moved to resettlement areas provided by the government. Ayan and her mother moved to the Loob-Bunga resettlement, where they have had to adjust to a new life. Their one-room house is made of bamboo and covered with palm leaves. Like many rural families, they have little furniture and sleep on mats on the floor at night. They cook their meals over a wood fire and wash their laundry in a nearby river.

Mothers in the resettlement village often wash young children outside in the warm sun.

Ayan and her mother at their home

Five mornings a week, Nic and Ely walk to their school in the resettlement village. Before classes begin, they gather outside with their classmates. They sing the Philippine national anthem while the flag is raised.

At most Filipino schools, classrooms are built around a large open space for playing. The classrooms have big windows and doors, which are left open to allow cool breezes to pass through.

Education is highly valued in the Philippines. Most children go to school and nearly all learn to read and write. Classes are quite large, with up to 40 students. Sometimes there are not enough books, paper, and pencils to go around.

Students study subjects such as math, science, history, government, English, and Pilipino. They also take home economics classes that teach practical skills such as sewing and cooking. Many schools have a vegetable garden where students learn about farming.

Nic and Ely on their way home from school

During recess, students jump rope and play games outside.

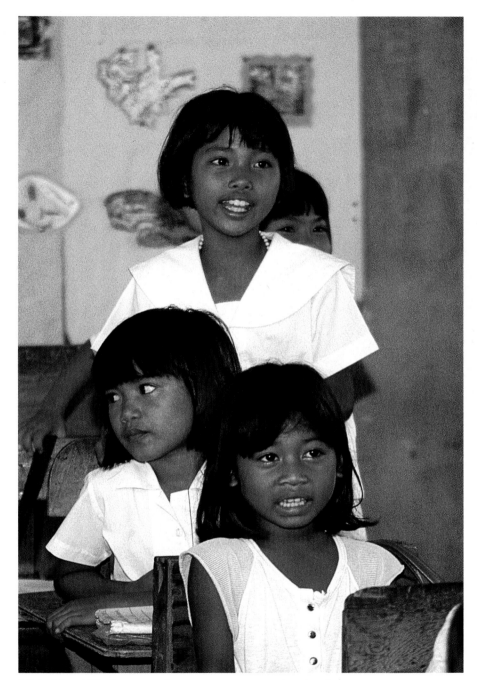

Nic's friend Thelma stands to answer a question in class.

Many Filipino students wear uniforms to school. Early in the morning and in the afternoon, the streets of many towns and villages are flooded with children in their brightly colored uniforms.

Every day, Bernadette and her brother Benedict ride the bus together to school in Camiling on the island of Luzon. From an early age, they were taught to look out for each other.

In general, Filipino families are very close. It is quite common for three generations of a family to live together under the same roof. Parents teach their children to have good manners and to respect their elders. Those values are also taught at school, and teachers receive the same respect that parents do.

Bernadette says she is glad to have a big brother who can help her with her homework. She and Benedict try not to fight with each other or with their parents and grandparents, who live with them.

Many students in the Philippines wear uniforms to school.

To shield themselves from the hot sun or from heavy rains, some children carry umbrellas as they walk to school.

Students and teachers pay John to bring them home from school on his tricycle.

On the southern island of Negros, sixteen-year-old John takes students to school on his tricycle. A tricycle is a motorcycle with a sidecar and a roof that shields passengers from the sun and rain. John works from sunrise to sunset almost every day. Up to twelve passengers can ride on his tricycle at one time. Since many Filipinos cannot afford cars or trucks, tricycles are used to carry just about anything that will fit.

Another popular form of transportation in the Philippines is the pedicab. A pedicab is a bicycle with a carriage attached to it. In the city of Jolo, pedicabs wind their way through the streets. There are very few cars in Jolo, but pedicabs often get caught in pedicab traffic jams. Teenagers pedal the pedicabs to earn money.

Tricycles are used to carry just about anything—even pigs on the way to market.

Most people in the city of Jolo get around in pedicabs.

In the city of Bacolod on the island of Negros, Filipinos of all ages look forward to the Masskara Festival, which takes place every October. At a festival, or fiesta, people celebrate a religious holiday or other special event.

At the Masskara Festival, people enjoy parades, dancing, games, and a variety of food. The festival takes its name from two words: *mass,* which means "many," and *cara,* the Spanish word for "face." *Masskara* refers to both masks and many faces.

Music and voices from the loudspeaker in the city square can be heard many blocks away. On the festival's final day, a huge street parade is held. The mayor of Bacolod welcomes the crowd and applauds local school bands as they march by.

Ferdinand enjoys trying on a mask. The smiling mask is the symbol of the Masskara Festival.

Luis gets help adjusting his drum before marching with his school band in the parade.

For many young people in Bacolod, marching in the parade is the highlight of the Masskara Festival.

To weave cloth, Elsa uses colored cotton thread on a machine called a loom.

South of Bacolod, on the southern tip of the island of Mindanao is the city of Zamboanga. The scent of orchids and other tropical flowers fills the air. Colorful displays of flowers, fish, vegetables, fruits, and clothing decorate Zamboanga's popular market. The market opens early in the morning and bustles with activity all day. Filipinos living in small cities and towns do most of their shopping in outdoor and indoor marketplaces.

In a village outside Zamboanga, Elsa and her family weave scarves, table mats, and clothing. They sell these items to tourists at the city market. Many girls growing up in tribal villages begin learning how to weave at a young age.

Elsa belongs to a tribal group called the Yakan. The Yakan women and girls are well known for their beautiful weaving. They use their own unique patterns and colors.

Zamboanga's market offers many colorful items.

This young girl practices basic weaving skills.

Aziz

Aziz lives in the heart of Zamboanga. Every day he comes home from school for lunch with his family. Today, because they are having guests, Aziz's grandmother has made a special meal of cooked vegetables, steamed rice, grilled fish, red crabs, and a sour soup called *sinigang*. Papayas and bananas are served for dessert.

Like many people in the southern Philippine Islands, Aziz and his family practice the Muslim religion. Aziz's father runs a school for Muslim children on the nearby island of Jolo. Amina and Nageeb attend the school, where they study the Koran, the Muslim holy book. Their mother walks them to class each day.

Amina and Nageeb with their mother at school

Aziz's grandmother has cooked a special meal for the family's guests.

41

In the nearby village of Campo Islam, Yuzhra awakens at 5:00 A.M. every morning to the sound of the prayer call. Like most Muslims, she and her brothers and sisters begin their day by praying. They face west, in the direction of the Muslim holy city Mecca, in Saudi Arabia. Yuzhra prays in Arabic, the language of the Koran.

Yuzhra is eighteen and works as a midwife. She helps mothers deliver their babies. Most women living in rural areas of the Philippines have their babies at home and not in hospitals. Yuzhra has helped deliver forty babies in all.

Yuzhra helps take care of her brothers and sisters.

The Muslim place of worship is called a mosque. The call to prayer comes from a tall tower called a minaret.

Yuzhra looks through a photo album in her bedroom.

As daylight begins to fade, children all over the Philippines help their families finish the day's work. When work is done, children gather to play games such as basketball and *piko,* or hopscotch. Others do their homework for the next day.

For children in the Philippines, this is a time of hope and change. Many young people now living on family farms may one day live in the city. Others growing up in a traditional, tribal lifestyle may have to choose between preserving traditions and adopting a new, more modern, way of life. While the children of the Philippines face many challenges, they continue to be hopeful and to work hard for a better future.

After school, Mellan and Cecilia relax on a wall near their home in northern Luzon. Both girls say they want to live in a big city when they grow up.

Piko, *or hopscotch, is a popular game on the beach.*

44

The children of the Philippines face the future with hope and the strength of their traditions.

Pronunciation Guide

Aeta EYE-tah
Bacolod bah-KOH-lahd
Baguio BAH-ghee-oh
banca BAHNG-kah
barangay bah-rahng-GUY
Batad BAH-tahd
carabao kah-rah-BAW-oo
Ifugao ee-poo-GAW-oo
Jolo HOH-loh
Luzon loo-ZAHN
Manila muh-NIL-uh
Mindanao min-duh-NAW-oo
Mount Pinatubo mount pin-uh-TOO-boh
Negros NAY-grohs
Sagada sah-GAH-dah
sinigang sih-nih-GAHNG
Sual swahl
tae kwon do tie kwahn doh
Yakan yah-KAHN
Zamboanga zam-BWAHNG-guh

Index

Photo Credits:
Additional photos courtesy of: Bettmann Archive, p. 8; Official USAF Photo
by SRA Paul Davis, p. 26.